Looking at . . . Plesiosaurus

A Marine Reptile from the JURASSIC Period

THE NEW
DINOSAUR
COLLECTION

For a free color catalog describing Gareth Stevens' list of high-quality books, call 1-800-542-2595 (USA) or 1-800-461-9120 (Canada). Gareth Stevens' Fax: (414) 225-0377.

Library of Congress Cataloging-in-Publication Data

Amery, Heather.
    Looking at— Plesiosaurus / written by Heather Amery ; illustrated by Tony Gibbons. — North American ed.
       p. cm. — (The New dinosaur collection)
    Includes index.
    ISBN 0-8368-1278-6
    1. Plesiosaurus—Juvenile literature. [1. Plesiosaurus. 2. Dinosaurs.] I. Gibbons, Tony, ill. II. Title. III. Title: Plesiosaurus. IV. Series.
QE862.P4A44 1995
567.9'3—dc20   94-36808

This North American edition first published in 1995 by
Gareth Stevens Publishing
1555 North RiverCenter Drive, Suite 201
Milwaukee, Wisconsin 53212 USA

This U.S. edition © 1995 by Gareth Stevens, Inc. Created with original © 1994 by Quartz Editorial Services, Premier House, 112 Station Road, Edgware HA8 7AQ U.K.

Consultant: Dr. David Norman, Director of the Sedgwick Museum of Geology, University of Cambridge, England.

Additional artwork by Clare Herronneau.

Printed in the United States of America

1 2 3 4 5 6 7 8 9 99 98 97 96 95

Looking at . . . Plesiosaurus

A Marine Reptile from the JURASSIC Period

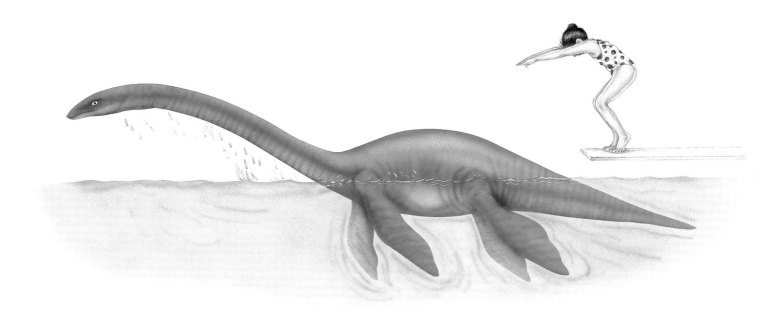

by Heather Amery

Illustrated by Tony Gibbons

THE NEW
DINOSAUR
COLLECTION

Gareth Stevens Publishing
MILWAUKEE

Contents

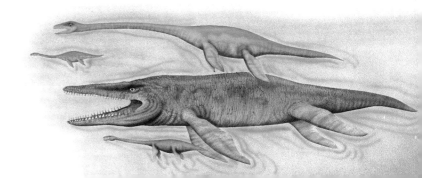

Introducing
Plesiosaurus

This creature, with its long, snakelike neck and round body, swam in the prehistoric oceans. Known as **Plesiosaurus** (PLEE-ZEE-OH-SAW-RUS), it was given this name, which means "near-reptile," because scientists thought it resembled a reptile.

About 200 million years ago, in Early Jurassic times, **Plesiosaurus** spent all its life in water. Was it intelligent? How large was it? What did it eat? And could any **Plesiosaurus** still be alive today?

Join us in a great underwater expedition to take a closer look at these extraordinary beasts.

It was not a typical reptile, however, because of its unusual shape.

Plesiosaurus lived in the sea during the same time many of the early dinosaurs lived on land. That's why it is featured in *The New Dinosaur Collection*.

5

Sea monster

Plesiosaurus was about 10 feet (3 meters) long — about the length of a small car. It had an amazing neck and a round, barrel-shaped body. One scientist described it as a snake threaded through a turtle! But you are unlikely ever to see a live one because scientists believe they died out over 170 million years ago.

Plesiosaurus first appeared about 200 million years ago and lived in what is now southern and central England. One of the first complete fossilized skeletons was found by a woman, Mary Anning, in 1814.

She discovered **Plesiosauru**s in soft, crumbling cliffs near a town called Lyme Regis in the southern county of Dorset.

These strange creatures swam in shallow seas, lagoons, and riverbeds. But, although they spent their lives in water, the same way fish do, they breathed air just like land animals.

No one knows for sure how **Plesiosaurus** gave birth because no fossilized remains of eggs or babies have ever been found. But some scientists think **Plesiosaurus** laid eggs, like turtles do today. Using her flippers, a mother would dig a hole in the sand and lay her eggs in it.

Next, she would cover them with sand, leaving them to hatch in the heat of the sun. The babies would find their own way to the water. But they had to watch out. There were plenty of large monsters in the sea.

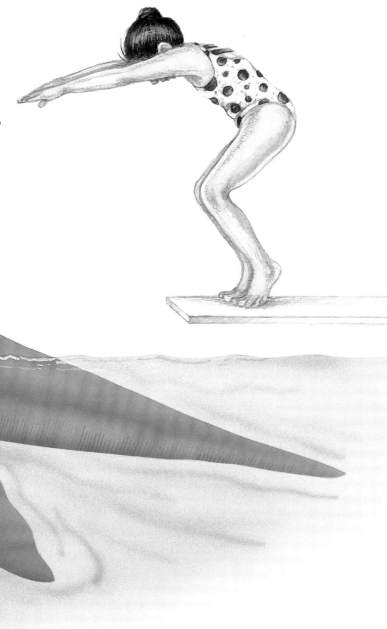

Inside Plesiosaurus

Take a look at this **Plesiosaurus** skeleton. What stands out most of all is its great, long neck with a huge number of bones that fit neatly together. At the end of the neck, you can see a small skull with rows of sharp teeth.

This prehistoric sea creature was an active hunter, and its flexible neck helped it change direction quickly when pursuing its prey.

Plesiosaurus had a round body with thick ribs. Four flippers were

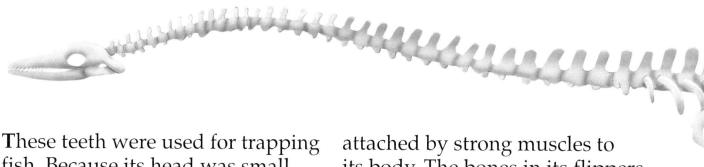

These teeth were used for trapping fish. Because its head was small, there was not much room for a brain, so chances are that **Plesiosaurus** was not very bright. But the sockets for its eyes were quite large, which probably means it had good eyesight. It could spot the approach of an enemy easily, as well as any delicious-looking fish for dinner.

attached by strong muscles to its body. The bones in its flippers were very much like the bones in your hands but much thicker and broader, and fused together. The hip and shoulder joints of **Plesiosaurus** show it had strong muscles. It could change the angle of its flippers as easily as you can twist and turn your hands.

Although **Plesiosaurus** had a big body, its lungs were probably smaller than those of a land animal of the same size. If its lungs had been any larger, **Plesiosaurus** would have just floated on the water's surface when the lungs were filled with air. It would not have been able to dive.

Scientists have found small stones in the stomachs of some fossilized skeletons of **Plesiosaurus**. It may have swallowed stones to weigh its

Notice how short its tail was when compared to its neck. Scientists have therefore decided **Plesiosaurus** was unlikely to use its tail to propel itself through the water. Its flippers and long neck were much more useful for swimming and darting around.

Scientists estimate the weight of a fully grown **Plesiosaurus** to have been about 2,200 pounds (1,000 kilograms) — that's about 14 times as heavy as an average adult human today. Even though it was not the largest sea creature of its time, **Plesiosaurus** was still huge by today's standards.

body down so it could float lower in the water. Some scientists also believe **Plesiosaurus** used the stones to grind up tough food in its stomach.

The Jurassic ocean

All sorts of reptiles swam in the warm, shallow Jurassic ocean — searching for food, chasing schools of fish, and crunching on shells.

Some of these sea reptiles were harmless.

Others were like giant crocodiles and had huge jaws lined with sharp teeth.

10

The Jurassic ocean was a lively and sometimes dangerous place. Even **Plesiosaurus** had to keep a careful lookout for any larger predators that might be lurking.

How did it swim?

Plesiosaurus swam through the warm Jurassic ocean, weaving its neck from side to side in search of fish and other marine creatures to eat. It moved slowly and gracefully, using its four flexible flippers.

These four flippers were thick and strong. **Plesiosaurus** moved them like wings, flapping them up and down to move along at a gentle speed in the water.

Turning its flippers, it could dive in the water, coming up to the surface again three or four times an hour to breathe.

As you can see, **Plesiosaurus** must have looked very graceful as it swam.

It must have been a champion diver, too, often plunging back into the sea to chomp on water plants and snap up fish.

Underwater adventure

Plesiosaurus was hungry and on the lookout for a meal. Twisting its head from side to side, it was searching for something tasty.

Suddenly, **Plesiosaurus** saw an appetizing squid disappear behind a rock. **Plesiosaurus** snaked out its long neck and began to swim toward it.

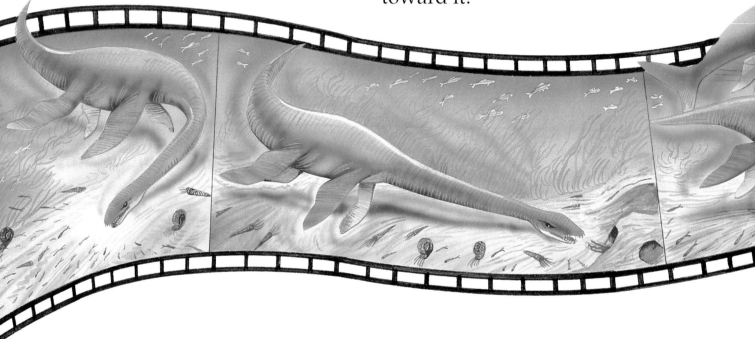

Diving down, it paddled through the water plants on the shallow seabed. Here, shrimplike animals and small fish scurried around the rocks.

Just as **Plesiosaurus** opened its jaws, ready to snap, it felt a rushing movement in the water. It turned its head and saw the long, dark shape of an enemy.

It was an **Ichthyosaurus** (IK-THEE-OH-SAW-RUS), also speeding toward the squid! **Plesiosaurus** thrust itself forward with its flippers, trying to reach the squid first. But the **Ichthyosaurus** swam swiftly, lashing with its tail and pushing **Plesiosaurus** aside with its body.

Struggling hard, **Plesiosaurus** managed to wrench itself away from the jaws of the predator but left a chunk of its own flesh behind. Ouch! It squealed in pain.

Slowly, **Plesiosaurus** swam away, blood from its wound coloring the water. That **Ichthyosaurus** bite would take time to heal.

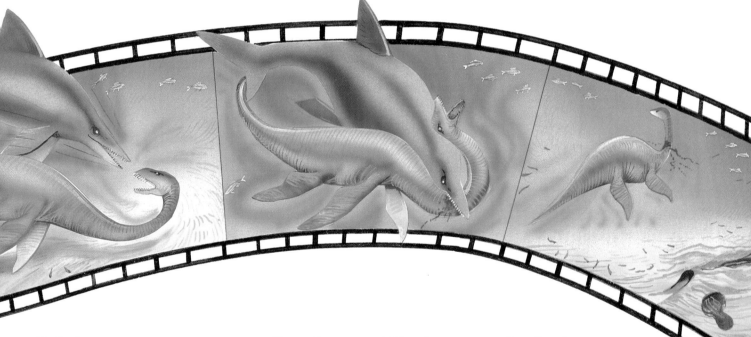

Ichthyosaurus was a reptile, about the same size as **Plesiosaurus**, and it had a body like a dolphin. It swam very fast and had long jaws armed with many sharp, peglike teeth. Suddenly, it sprang up and attacked. **Plesiosaurus** shuddered in fright. It had not expected its squid hunt to end in a battle.

Plesiosaurus looked around, in case it could warn others that a dangerous creature was nearby. It had lost the battle with the **Ichthyosaurus**, and the lucky squid had escaped. **Plesiosaurus** would have to find another meal when it felt a little better.

Is Plesiosaurus

For thousands of years, there have been stories of huge monsters living in lakes. People claim to have seen them in Scotland, Canada, the United States, Ireland, Norway, and Chile. They have names such as Slimy Sid, Ogopogo, Pooka, the Hvaler Serpent, and White Lake Monster.

Probably the best-known is the Loch Ness Monster of Scotland. *Nessie*, as it is often called, is supposed to live in this very deep loch, or lake, that was joined to the North Sea back in prehistoric times.

Hundreds of people say they have spotted Nessie coming up from the water. A fuzzy, black-and-white photograph was taken of it in 1934.

alive today?

The snapshot showed a monster with a long neck moving through the loch. Scientists figured out how big it was and how fast it was moving from this picture. Some even suggested it was a **Plesiosaurus** that had survived after others had become extinct. But they had been fooled.

In 1994, the photograph was found to be a fake. The "monster" was, in fact, a trick photograph of a toy submarine.

Many people who live near the loch still say they have seen *something* in the water, however, even though underwater cameras have found no real evidence.

Which dinosaurs could swim?

While **Plesiosaurus** swam in the sea, dinosaurs lived on dry land. But, although none of the dinosaurs lived in water, scientists think some may have plunged into lakes and rivers to catch food and escape predators.

Some dinosaurs actually went into the water to feed. **Baryonyx** (BAH-REE-ON-ICKS), for example, lived about 120 million years ago and paddled in shallow water in what is now England. It caught fish in its long, hooked claws or snapped at the fish with its huge jaws, in the same way crocodiles do today.

Maiasaura (MY-A-SAW-RA), *opposite center*, was about as long as a city bus and lived 75 million years ago. Huge herds of this dinosaur roamed the plains of what is now Montana, feeding on plants and low trees.

Maiasaura had no sure way of defending itself against the large meat-eating dinosaurs, such as **Tyrannosaurus rex** (TIE-<u>RAN</u>-OH-<u>SAW</u>-RUS RECKS), *top*.

When frightened by them, **Maiasaura** may have run into a river or lake. Paddling with its front legs and waggling its tail, it would try to swim away from danger with all its strength.

Brachiosaurus (<u>BRACK</u>-EE-OH-<u>SAW</u>-RUS), *below*, was one of the biggest and heaviest dinosaurs that ever lived.

It had a huge body and a neck so long it could stretch over the roof of a three-story house. It would occasionally plod into lakes and rivers to browse on plants growing along the banks.

With its great, long neck, **Brachiosaurus** could easily stretch its head out to eat a wide variety of plants.

19

Plesiosaurus data

Flipper feet
Under the water, **Plesiosaurus** would flap its four limbs, using its strong muscles to help it swim. By turning these flippers, it could dive down to the bottom of the shallow sea and come up again. Its toes were webbed together on each flipper foot and looked like a mitten.

Snakelike neck
Plesiosaurus had a long, flexible neck that it would shoot out to catch passing fish. Under the water, **Plesiosaurus** used its neck to help it twist and turn its body when swimming.

With its long neck and round body, **Plesiosaurus** would have been easy to spot as it swam. Its small head would show above the water as it came up to breathe from time to time.

Barrel-shaped body

Plesiosaurus had a large, round body that looked like a barrel. It was so heavy it could not push very quickly through the water to escape from the large, meat-eating monsters that swam in the prehistoric seas. Predators would have chased **Plesiosaurus** eagerly to get a meal of its flesh. The barrel-like belly of **Plesiosaurus** probably looked particularly appetizing.

Overlapping teeth

This swimming reptile had rows of teeth that overlapped when it closed its jaws. These teeth acted like a trap for catching fish. Once inside, a fish could not escape, and the **Plesiosaurus** was sure of its meal.

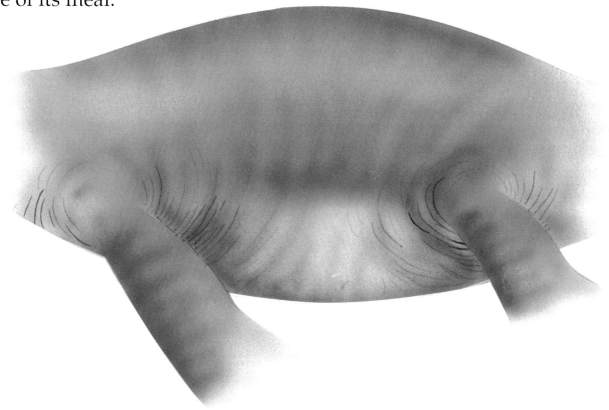

The Plesiosaur gang

Plesiosaurus (**1**) was small in comparison to others in the **Plesiosaur** family. These marine reptiles lived in oceans, rivers, and lakes from Early Jurassic times, about 200 million years ago, to near the end of Cretaceous times, about 70 million years ago.

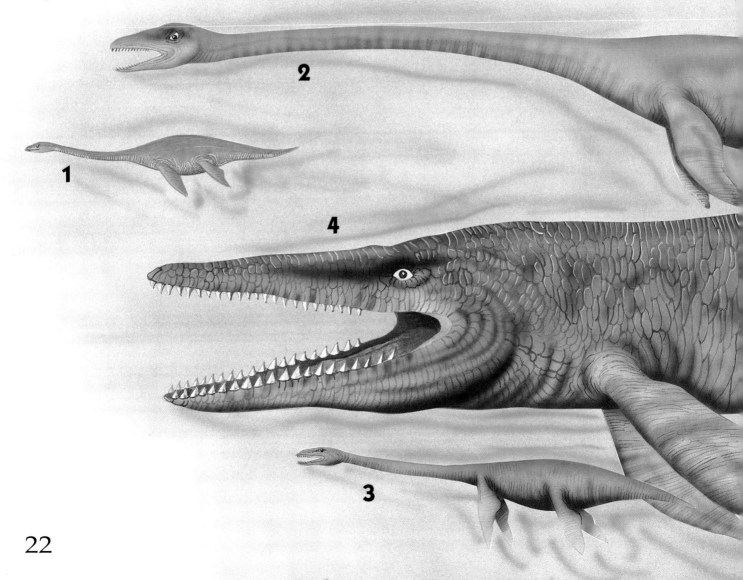

Many other, much larger **Plesiosaurs** swam in the seas at that time. Let's meet some of them.

Remains of **Elasmosaurus** (EE-LASS-MOE-SAW-RUS) (**2**) have been found in western North America. Its name means "ribbon reptile," and it lived about 70 million years ago. This "sea serpent" was about the length of two city buses. Its head was small but had many sharp teeth — all the better to gobble up unsuspecting marine creatures.

Cryptoclidus (KRIP-TOE-KLY-DUS) (**3**) lived about 170 million years ago in Jurassic times. Fossilized skeletons have been found only in southern England. It was just about 13 feet (4 m) long, with a very small head. When its jaws closed, the teeth overlapped. This strange bite made a useful fish trap.

Kronosaurus (KRONE-OH-SAW-RUS) (**4**) was another relative of **Plesiosaurus**. It only had a short neck, but its jaws were huge, and it had teeth. It grew to about 56 feet (17 m) long and probably ate other **Plesiosaurs**, as well as fish and other reptiles. It lived in Cretaceous times in the ocean waters that now surround Australia.

GLOSSARY

expedition — a journey or voyage.

extinction — the dying out of all members of a plant or animal species.

flippers — wide, flat limbs some animals use for swimming.

fossils — traces or remains of plants and animals found in rock.

marine — living in or formed by the ocean or sea.

predators — animals that capture and kill other animals for food.

prey — animals that are captured and killed for food by other animals.

propel — to make something move in a forward direction.

remains — a skeleton, bones, or a dead body.

reptiles — cold-blooded animals that have hornlike or scale-covered skin.

INDEX